We Live in Bodies

Also by Ellen Doré Watson

The Alphabet in the Park: Selected Poems of Adélia Prado
(translations)
WESLEYAN UNIVERSITY PRESS, 1990

Broken Railings
(Green Lake Chapbook Prize)
OWL CREEK PRESS, 1996

For the two Adelias,

Adélia Luzia Prado de Freitas & Adelia Doré Jenkins

Acknowledgments

Grateful acknowledgment is made to the editors of the following journals in which poems from *We Live in Bodies* have appeared, some in earlier versions:

Boulevard: "Where the Dead Live"
Field: "E=mc²" and "Funny How"
Many Mountains Moving: "The Body Speaks"
The Marlboro Review: "Circa 1970"
The Massachusetts Review: "Once"
The New Yorker: "Glen Cove, 1957"
The Pioneer Valley Forum: "Wafer"
Ploughshares: "Liza" and "Now That the Fields"
Poetry Northwest: "Anything But Empty" and "Gone Fishin'"
   (winner of the magazine's Bullis-Kizer Prize)
Sanctuary, The Journal of the Massachusetts Audubon Society: "May at
   the Agway"

Four of these poems are included in a chapbook entitled *Broken Railings*, which won the Green Lake Chapbook Prize (Owl Creek Press, 1996).

"A Hotel by Any Other Name" appeared in *Night Out: Poems about Hotels, Motels, Restaurants, and Bars* (Milkweed Editions, 1997).

"What Gets Left OEpigraph from "A Man Inhabited a House" by Adélia Prado is from *The Alphabet in the Park: Selected Poems of Adélia Prado*, 1990 by Wesleyan University Press / University Press of New England ut of History Books" is included in *This Wood Sang Out*, an anthology produced by The Literacy Project (1995).

With gratitude to Doug Anderson for the belief and the jumpstart
To Carlen Arnett for inspired editing and shaping
To the "No Rules" peer group for champagne & nitty-gritty
To the writers in my workshops, who sustain and inspire
To Barbara Ras, first and best sister-writer
And to Paul Jenkins, daily, making everything possible

"The Body experiences joy, the tongue eats it:
bright, hot, unquestionable as suns.
Do we die?
I understand mathematics better."

—Adélia Prado

Contents

THREE

FOUR

ONE

Wafer

Why on a perfectly crisp January day did you change
your month-old arrangement of cells and simply
dissolve into nothingness like a communion wafer
in one more sinner's mouth?   Finally, to have a seed
take root inside the part of me I never learned
to own, finally after so many graphs and new months'
blood, so many folded hands sprouting from white
sleeves over desktops, so many reverent moments after sex
with the bowl of me tipped up and waiting, a nest
of twenty minutes, as he tilted a water glass to my lips
how many times before sleep, and now—four slim weeks
after you became a matter of blessed fact, a euphoric
knot of nausea I sat hugging, grinning my goofy
we beat the odds grin—to have you dead in there,
a bit of the bit you are leaking down my thigh:
how could you leave us here, two people with every reason
to rage and no one to call cruel?

It Will Take How Long

1

My father's sermons lasted twenty minutes. Finally
we get to sing the last hymn. Ten-thousand-sixty minutes
until the next possible funny story featuring me
or my brothers. Time is like money: grown-ups
control it. Worms and their bloody pulp
on wet asphalt, all because adults hurry so—
except when they're locked in the long tube
their voices make. Think of the wait
before they notice a child can pour her own milk
—and the way they calibrate the shaky
white flow of confidence. Time is not kind
to children except when they sleep. Are we
there yet? Am I me yet? It will take
how long to build this mirror?

2

It takes as long to cook black beans as to drive to the shore. It
takes as long to sweat as to blink. As long to weed the garden
as you have. It takes as long to fall in love as to fall out. I can
iron six shirts in four commercials. It takes as long for the sun
to creep across the rug to my thigh as it does for me to decide
not to tell one brother what the other has said. As long for the
bud to open as she took dying. It takes me longer to wake than
to fall asleep. Thoughts rise up and brush past cobwebs, too soft
to set a rhythm. The beans are done.

3

I can part time like filmy curtains, or slap it aside—
any strategy so as not to get stuck. It's taken a long
necklace of years to learn this. Everything but our pagan,
automatic breathing is a choice we make in time
or time makes for us. Are you facing yourself or a door?
I have complained away a lot of years, handed over time-flesh
out of fear, and received no crystal treasure in return.
An afternoon is as easy to lose as your sense of satisfaction.
I take smaller bites now and love them to my heart. I try
to take each new day's clock for what it is—toy, a weapon,
a hunk of junk. Could be invisible. Could be dinner.
To be in the place that I am. The curve of skin,
the warbly-noted dark thread of the edible now.

What Gets Left Out of History Books

after Thomas Lux

Tenderness rarely appears. People don't sigh.
There's no burping. In history books the human music
gets shouted out by clashing metal and swell-headed ideas.
Reading, we forget that babies were born as bombs fell,
that the first newspapers were gaped at by many unlettered
eyes, we never hear how Mr. Big's Mom refused him her breast
at three months but baked him a linzer torte before every
major speech. Frank's idea for an electric engine didn't
work, so we never heard about his blindness in later life.
The children in these pages wear distended bellies or tiny
crowns; they sing under a spotlight or lie in mass graves.
Where are the peach trees, the pies? Where are you and I?

Sleep with the Face of an Axe

We sleep in ones and twos always singly
We sleep and most of us waken
We sleep in the opera, in the blue curl of snowdrift
Sleep offers forgetfulness cupped in his hand
Sleep eats it and chortles, sends us back
haunted or healed

She sleeps with a note under her pillow—
Mama's first apology—and baby rabbits
he with a trigger, fingers looped round and ready
I sleep with a number on auto-dial
a belated answer, any answer
sleeping to find the question, loving the sleep
that floods me invisible, loving also
caveman sleep and me upside down on his shoulder

Sleep finds my heart almost anywhere
fills it with arched faces, dark corners, lost etchings
Sleep rolls us down the chute into hairshirts
of our own making: fires, reasons to run,
inexplicable nakedness, my once-a-week dream-plane
rolling up to its pleated sleeve with me still
50 miles away watering the cat, fingering underwear
and shoes, never the right shoes
Sleep's where the knife-thrust comes out of nowhere
on the median strip, on the bias
What does it mean that hardly anyone eats
in their dreams and that I'm the exception
You'd think I'd know better than to wonder why
You'd think we'd think twice
before lying down, asking for more
but sleep is where Frankie's still 18 and never got married
where friendship won out over money

sleep, our prehistoric home, land of the instant replay
habitual miracle of oblivion

Handsome trickster, faithless mate
brute with a heart of alfalfa
sleep appears on the fault lines of day or night
on trains, surrounded by algebra
with or without our knowledge
spray of light that knows how to deepen
handwritten invite to the dark folds of mushrooms
subtle as slow rain on leaves and as green
Come, sleep with the face of an axe, breath
of gardenia, I am ready—
but let this not be the last—

Dream Tales from the Barn

The white rooster is too new at this,
too newly glorious, victorious, to notice
how the west wind has flattened
its hand against the barnboards.

Yesterday's hero, name of Choochoo,
still flaunting the sheen of his plumage
minus the prize green tail feathers, waiting
for his red crest to rise bravely
from the ashes of frostbite,
has taken it all in, flat wind and flimsy wood,
but he's too busy stewing about the hens
gone over to the other side, and the bald spot
on his back pecked larger by the day.

The flea-bitten brown cock who never stood a chance,
never sees the light of day, sits drilled into his lonely corner,
smugly aware of the wind's highly organized goings-on,
cheering for it in his sad, airless heart, waiting
for the barn to cave in on a wild feathered frenzy,
waiting for the dust to settle, one chance in three.

The Ones

We sit staring at our hands, fear-driven.
Black with newsprint, we're up to our eyebrows
in the refrain (our only solace): *they're not
like we are.* The ones who put match to paper
or wear bones through their lips, the ones who fall

from greatness into the net of celebrity lawyers.
The ones who listen to brass. The ones sleeping
in messy pieces under headstones, the ones who can
yodel. People with no asphalt leading to their doors,
whose feet take them where they need to go, or

people with trust funds or bagpipes or exit wounds.
We could keep this up, but our we is shrinking.
Lift up a stone, find a work ethic to rival ours.
Think of all the fat men in sunglasses who have
buttons to push. What about the guys with full body

tattoos or dusty brown uniforms? Or the little people
who stay up all night rearranging the borders?
I agree, I don't like the way they flatten their a's,
the unbreathable fabric they wear, but you
don't know the first thing about syllables.

Relations in high places? Any twin can become an exile,
just bring money into the mix. You know what they say:
intermarriage brings on a case of sore buns
from fence-sitting. Some clubs you choose, some
there's no way to lose. So how do we shape a we

from frayed nerves and incompatible diets? How
to avoid committing genocide when we feel so short?
Too little rain to remain an island, so always keep

one hand free. Be intimate with strangers. Your life
is in all of our hands. When sameness begins closing in,

get out the spyglass, bring on the Pogo sticks.
Wear welcome mats for clothes. We're becalmed,
dust bunnies! We're in a tippy boat and muck's the rule.
Take off your shoes and eat some greens.
It's a big we.

Monday Morning Paper

Maybe she hit the twins sometimes—Lord,
two pairs of them under six—when four open
mouths had to be stopped, when looking
at them reminded her what she couldn't build
in two rooms with only paper, scissors,
rock. Maybe early on he made ownership look
attractive, showing her off like a new boat.
At first with those big hands he could rock
a frayed life to happy slumber, but he idled
rough. He tanked and roughed her up and those
four pairs of eyes helped her roll him out
the door and a judge said for good.
                                        Yesterday
he came back—because he wanted to, how could
paper stop him. Rock sharpens scissors and no one
seems surprised they were sharp. Four pairs of eyes
watched his thick right arm flail its answer on her chest
and when finally someone came, the smallest one
asked: *Did he get Mommy's heart?*

Battered Toddler, Page B6

Sometimes grown-ups forget you're down there
on the floor with the ant traps and loose wiring.
It would be wise not to chew either one. Daddy
will wake from his stupor, Mommy will tire
of her old Sinatras. Best to forgive them now,
before it gets worse; that way you'll have some
forgiveness left for later. When they remember
they're parents, you'll have a better shot at Kix
or popsicles or Daddy's keys if they find you
wearing a funny hat instead of shredding papers
at the mail slot. If they wake and go
straight to the medicine cabinet or each other's
throats, grab a fuzzy and get scarce. Put your
tears and shrieks into the cheap blue fur.
When their eyes happen to fall on you the moment
they hate themselves the most (you can smell it),
you must play very but not too dead. Try to
leave your body in their hands—without it
you can climb to the window ledge and look out.
Just don't forget the way back inside your bruised
skin, you will need to take it with you if you find
a time to run, or tell. If they beat all the life
out of you, red dragonflies with wings half air,
half spun gold, gazillions of them, will rise up
and bear you to the warm basket waiting
beside the stove of God. Well. Whatever death
turns out to be, it will be one good mother.

Circa 1970

For David Kunz

I think I thought if I could convince you there was a tiny cup
nestled in the red folds under your sternum, holding the vast
store of your goodness, I thought if I could make you see
you had opened me, lifting the wig from its hairpins
and my girl-self with it, if you could know and believe
that while they wired and shocked you I was home breathing in
your blue workshirt, that my needing your smell on my skin
contained more electricity, would rearrange your brain cells
the way the doctors meant to, then you would come back to me
and the beat-up Falcon and the hundred pound bag of brown rice
in the back seat and know you deserved us, such as we were.

But your grandmother had taped the walls of your childhood
with newspaper, bits of tin foil with thumbtacks, she triple-
wrapped you and the leftovers and kept your saucer-eyed
mother in a little box. Your father, they said, disappeared
when she asked for a new refrigerator and she has talked little
since. No wonder you wanted us shabby, left the A & P grinning
(stolen t-bones in your motorcycle helmet), and ducked
into the darkroom to watch faces form from blurs. It's because
of you that I choose the troubled light, the uneasy breeze.
Because of you I do not button buttons or scour corners,
I choose to vote for skin and dirt. I think

if I could have convinced you I felt safe
even when you held the knife, you would be loving
someone now, not sitting in some hole or hospital sunk in a chair
lit by TV. But in all those years I discovered no way
to reach into your body and show you the glowing,

you were so fervent doubting the part of me I was most sure of
in Allston and Port Angeles and on the road and in my skin
and that was you.

You Know Who You Are

There are at least six of you whose pasts I want to smash,
judge and jury, cruel and unusual: foolish do-gooder,
once I get a look inside the people I want you to hate
I see the bloom of shadows at their shoulders, an accordion
of black paper dolls, hand to hand to hand to the horizon,
and I have to quick make more tears.

At least one of you taught me: it's not a monster in us
that needs killing, not our parents; it's weakness
turned violet over time, sprouting backwards and forwards,
haphazard, scattershot. Oh, we are so much smaller
than the cruelty in our bodies—the stubborn root
life finds a way to water almost always.

There are at least four of you I want to worship, four souls
done with smashing: one who looks in the mirror at her child eyes
and sees, one who opens his chest, pulls out the rage to wound
and breaks it down into words; one finds a way to paint,
another to mourn. If I pray, it will be to you who find a way
to live with a clenched fist and a clean heart.

$E = mc^2$

My foot on the gas pedal says yes and goes on gassing
        while the electric hairnet under my scalp tingles
a warning. Matter can be crammed with marbleized yes-and-no,
        a zigzag greater than the sum of its parts.
You mean one thing, you do much more than another.
        Like the mailman's son: giddy, celebrating his new house,
he put the gun to his ear at the barbeque and it's loaded, bang.
        Hey, I've fallen asleep at the wheel, haven't you?
What about the woman—turned out it was me—giving a whack to a
        two-year-old, way against policy. Up through my *bon vivant*
mood bubbled a mean swat naked among the baggage for all the airport
        and my stepdaughter to see. Oh, sweet clarity with nothing
written out in advance but the daily contradiction: a guy
        holed up in a house trailer, detox pamphlets on the table
and a pint on the bed. Nobody's betting. Is that a carsick cow
        nodding its sad head at my windshield or just two sides
of beef still as one, riding a truck to where they part company?
        Before I get a chance to consider the glass half-full of empty,
a stop sign—and a careening van. Who knows whose screech is whose,
        what color relativity. Unclear—but it's hurtling.

Great Blue

The day she's finally lucky enough to be standing in the driveway when the blue heron slices through everything invisible over her head, she feels the hairs on her arms come to attention and thinks that instead of grocery bags she should be holding a fencing foil or a large white calla lily. She eyes her neighbor's rampant bed of impatiens bobbing foolishly, red white red white, like those mustachioed heads goggling into their fuzzy necks on the back shelves of cars. She vows never to wear a hairdo that might be seen on a bank teller. She plays back the flight of the heron, searching its rhythmic wing beats for a sign—and surprises herself, unable to forgive that rare bird its elegance and singularity.

Her nipples want to drive all night to Alabama. Think about it: wouldn't the tent caterpillars just as soon not be eyesores? It's clear the crabapple tree with its elbows sawing back and forth at the least provocation is determined to corner the market on fiddle music and the neighborhood dogs are hell-bent on plucking each passing plane from the sky.

She sets down the groceries and bends to pick up the unremarkable stone that was meant to live in her pocket. Forgive us this day our unseemly aspirations. From the screen door across the August lawn there's a screech of pain, a pause, then uncertain laughter. The beech trees give a series of papery sighs and she wonders at the toughness of chlorophyll, so many teflon leaves battered but whole.

On the Seventh Anniversary of the Conception of My First Child

I look to the world. I ponder the possibility of number two.
   Out the window fresh nubs of dead wood suggest
putting on some lullabies and sitting on the front stoop
   to blow bubbles. The chickens with the wounds of winter
on their backs have tired of walking tiptoe in the mud.
   They long to do the cross-stitch in the grass; they're
dreaming of getting into real estate. It's a Spring thing.
   There's an attic full of baby clothes that want to get out.
They sigh and whisper with the rafters, *sell all your roadmaps—*
   hell, forget how to drive. I try to see myself as the eager
young poppy in the corner of the garden, always the first
   to wave her red hanky at each passing cloud. I rise like
dough on that childlike thought. I can shut out the checkbook
   crying me a river, and the bellyaching rooms, too full
to cough. What needles is this craving for another someone,
   for the pain and beauty of something tugging day and night,
something needy that has no words. Most days it's words I want.
   My eyes do their searching thing, but no skywriting in the high
thin air, no runes in the compost. The weather-beaten chicken shed
   is looking awfully sullen, playing it close to the vest. Soon darts
of green will gather at its ankles. We believe this on the flimsiest
   of evidence. Just as we know the scanty remains of the woodpile
and cluttered gutters will a take back seat to the question of those
   small boulders in the garden: are they saying goodbye, sucked
down under glacial mud, or rising up in the moonlight with a whiff
   of sour milk on their breath?

TWO

Liza

In the ambulance a child
is turning blue around the edges.
The sweep of time has lifted up her life
and we are a blur of hands trying
to refasten her to it. Two fingers
press a rhythm on her birdcage
chest. The muscle clenched inside
has a hole too wide. Time sweeps by
like wind. We sweep wind into her mouth
and her lips pink up. This allows us
to pretend she is alive. On the highway's
shoulder, doors flash open
to the Crit Team, to the clear bell
of a mother's calling. Our hands do
what they are told. We watch a man drill
a needle through to a small leg's marrow,
hear the chant from our mouths. We are inside
a tiny cell of time, far from the dull hallway
of hours and disbelief that will follow:
a toddler's groin—red, blue, yellow—
splayed open on a table in an airless room,
our hands thundering blanks in our laps,
our tongues so much paper in our mouths.

Natural Light

Her eyes flit open and stare hard at the ceiling,
all those little pebbles under the paint—what for?
His long body blinks awake beside her knowing
after fifty years together she hates the clock radio
again today, not for what it offers—tides, snipers,
botched elections—but for what it withholds
(not a single medical breakthrough for anyone near)
and she shivers *Let there be light*, presses her lashes
to their twin nests in her face like a long, dry prayer
Let this not be the day the center begins to blur.

It's more than the business of life that makes them rise
always in unison, just as their napping happens now
only in chairs, as if to avoid the jinx, the stray glimpse
of one eternally down, the other up and doing for both.
So she does and does, she clips and she pastes
standing guard over memory, coaxing away all the lint;
he's busy in the cellar where the sawdust rises
in the half-light beside his broom and he lets it.
He knows who the world and his wife think he is

and he wants her almost any way he can have her.
At noon she looks into the breadbox and sees
a hospital gown neatly folded and wrapped in plastic.
His feet are on the stairs and she will always know
even without eyes that they are his, big and blunt
like the hands she'll remember folded around his sandwich.
The bread tastes like cloth but she doesn't say so,
she thinks: if he were the kind of man to use the phrase
blind love he'd have to stop now, before things go dark.
He eats her leftover crusts and talks sense.

She looks at her watch, the band dissolves
into clear plastic, with her name and an unfamiliar number.

God said: Let there be age spots and there were.
She gasps and disowns the thought—remember Mrs. H,
how she let herself go?   Donuts and heartache—
once he's back downstairs, the sun moves into the room
and she heads for the drapes, catches a streak on the rug
that demands examining but no, nothing
faded here—this yellow is strong and slanting
on the floor where she never sets anything but her feet,

and suddenly she is sitting down on her sorry bones
feeling warmth through closed eyes.
Letting takes a long time.
Let the sweater unravel at its own speed at night and
stitch it up in the morning or be happy
fingering the yarn.
Let the darkness loom and it will let you climb it.
Whose words are these?   A breeze fills the house—
She lets it—

Hungry for Them

A year is a sausage held in by its own casing, linked
to those ahead and behind by a thin twist.
This requires a precise wrist action found
on the midway—man behind a mike in a silly hat
making balloon animals. His is an art beyond perfecting:
the rubber tubes squeak and hover uncertainly
between dog and cat, but still the children
wear his same fool smile. Why shouldn't years blurt by
in uneven homemade shapes?
                                        The year my *comadre*
curved into herself with a vengeance and froze, the year
angry boys turned our house on its head, walked away
with a picture of me six-months pregnant, naked and grinning—
surely that one was longer, more swollen with free radicals
than the year of our courting, or this last,
which left behind a warm loaf in place of fear. As if
our time of trial was over, as if the filo of peeling skin
would this time lift off in one piece, the fabric of self
intact for once for one thin year.
                                        No matter its girth
each year holds its breath at the last, tries to cinch in
its belly full of weaknesses, finally giving way to the next
amid a storm of good intentions. There are those who think
it's writ in some blue and holy place how many we get.
A year is a temporary shelter. We mustn't make too many holes
in the walls unless we're prepared to spackle. This
is what we have together. Better to suck than to chew.

The Long Road of Knowing

She didn't know hunger but had a bad case
of the wants. She knew the hymns, the ropes,
the service road. Self-denial was a virus,
she closed her mouth in its presence.
She was not good but *good at.* Her hands stumbled
their way to what would be her breasts, suddenly
white blouses had a purpose. She threw
her body through the air but was all legs
when it came to gliding. Somewhere around nylons
scruples slunk off to the crawl space and bravado
filled the gap. She knew they couldn't make her but not
how that would shape her: if cheating, if contempt,

then how love? If early warning system, how
generosity? Not that she'd have called it
karma, but she had a needling sense that things
were being lost in the sauce. It took living
in another language, it took growing a baby
to begin to get them back. Looking now over
her middle-aged shoulder it's the face of skinflint
time meandering down route 66. She thinks salt,
sees habit turned to landscape, fabric, present
imperfect. Sees how difficult undoing, how large
and ripe the now. She hums, trying to learn to be.
(A cup or a plate, not hands and a mouth.)

Emboldened by Love

There on the bedspread for the chambermaid to find:
the key to his heart. He had seen her only once,
from behind. Thin, ringed fingers dipping
into a thick braid, parting and loosening chestnut
waves to dance on her back. It was enough.
He was smitten, instantly. Only I lied. The *he*
was a *she*—no, an I. It felt like a lie at the time,
that desire. A dark yearning—not to make love
to that woman, but to inhabit her body, thinking
to love myself. She was not a chambermaid but
a pair of ears and a brain listening to poems.
Suddenly I noticed how she widened at the hips,
filling the wide-backed chair completely.
What a foolish complication, I thought, neither
welcome nor instructive. More like a hung jury,
an error message, a trial called on account of
rain. And still missing in action: my sense of me
as a boyish girl-child, bruised and graceless but
lanky. Back home, the heavy climb upstairs to bed.
A kiss and a look at my leggy wildflower, a sleeping
wonder cradling her childhood to her chest.
She moans and her arms fling open, one hand
falling on the lips between her legs.
I leave her to her buried treasure and find
my place beside the man who loves me mostly
as I am. Here in the bedclothes somewhere
for the finding: a key to unlock my body.

The Body Speaks

So? I'm a collection of oversized bones, blind in so much
casing, I'm a pair of lonely shoulders and a snip of a nose
turned up at the word cute. Two serious feet. Lungs
that have sworn off slang, still graced by old graffiti;
fingertips white candles that may never be lit. So what
if this voice has never learned how to huddle? This
is a mouth that leads, even on the dance floor.
This is a survivor of a liver, doing cartwheels down the yellow
line. These unmentionable thighs think they're in the wrong
movie, these are eyes that feast, ears for whispers. Two
nozzles of love that enjoy team sports and a wet spot
that would rather pay rent than sign papers. The bleached
walnut that thinks it's in charge keeps dozing off, keeps
to itself, wants to wash its hands of the question mark
—knees to mouth—in the baby space. This is a face
frontal by nature, too little set into too much. A belly
that bleeds for the world while it humps white food
unthinking, and hair that's easily disappointed. This body
has scars from cats and dogs and scalpels, a throbbing fist
of blood crucial as any other. The wrists alone remain
unchanged, sprouting plain-spoken hands that love
dirt today, satin tomorrow. So? Own it all—the walk-in vanity,
the basementful of self-disgust. As old as peekaboo: I loves me,
I loves me not. Oh, how the soul goes on trying to butter up
its wrapper. No choice but to live in this stew of mismatched
parts seasoned by doubt. Who needs the dumb self-assurance
of glaciers when you have love handles, when you have this
spacesuit for stroking they call skin? So, you know—play
with me. The way you do with words.

The Promise Dance

You stand in the hall screaming
        Lug nut! I might as well be a lug nut!
I duck behind the curtain
        moon with clouds veiling her cold kisses
You shrink back
        cold yellow with ways to fix things
I sink onto the sofa
        lady of sighs, a run in her hose
You find this promising
        thermostat up, lights down
I recall my promise
        slide to my side, drop the iron filings
You bring the dust pan
        a soft blanket, a side of you to remember
I offer myself, bra first
        to your two confident birds
You fly high and low
        hovercraft lover, till I'm wet and grooved
I release my swarm
        shoals of fish beneath the boat

What the Body Knows

Roof shingles melt in the afternoon sun, filling my eyes
with chocolate, and you want to know what could I live without
If I could never again smell almond, coconut, gardenia, the bed
                                        after love
If cilantro, arugula, papaya were no more than paper to my tongue
If no talking drums, no Sarah Vaughan, no rooster
If I couldn't feel the flat heat angling from the open sky, the cool
                                        green singing alto,
how could I blush and ripen like a pear in your hand
You lick your lips and ask which, of all senses, is the greatest treasure
and I say: her five-year-old vibrato, her exultant italicizing
of new words, the sweat rising from her part, the sight of her
                                        gleaming
in her sleep, the honey skin I could touch more
than I should, I do everything but taste her—

12 May 1996

Yes, we can loll here for six more chapters, before—yes,
waffles, yes you can stay naked all day or until you think
you need clothes, yes to butter on the video popcorn today
and me beside you for not just the scary parts, then yes
to a rain-walk, yes, even to the culvert rushing water and
the long way home, yes to candles with dinner, yes to no
lettuce, yes, I'll save the opera and switch to jazz, yes—
a bath bead?—take two, and yes I will sing the song, yes,
just this once, three times.

Anything But Empty

I don't remember the first crack and roll of labor,
just a sharp hum rising inside me, and Paul's night rattle.
The whole world locked up tight as a brick, and it's my time
to loosen. Wind carving wood; otherwise a great silence loud

with fear. Then, our two voices, rip and rap, static
in the tinder air. The door opens to the dark, a lone rooster
roused by the muffle of our leaving. The tires crunch
on the twenty-below road and every bump a winter knife.

In the back seat I try to borrow the dark and circle back
to our sex, to the twin oh's rushing from our throats,
the hollow he made for himself inside me, impossible
and wet. How our skin sang us to a roundness where something

might take hold. The moan swallowing me now is hard, I hate him
driving, hate the back of his doting head. In the hospital
we feel official, we forget music, forget oil for rubbing, this
pain will be productive. We can laugh now at the summertime

circle of blood, just a spot, a scare glistening between my legs,
our lips a chorus of no's and then the months going by, my hands
a clock splayed on a widening belly, warming to his cowboy songs.
Now he tells me gently that beyond these green walls light

is coming finally, slamming the parking lot for the long haul
and I must melt into the day of our birthing. I am at the bottom
of a well and everything is echo. I am lying on paper. I am huge
and cracking under the weight of these clocks, hordes of them

doing the scowl. Metal glints here and light is flat and
unrelenting. Outside the cold sun has given itself up once again
to the dark, and their eyes asking why can't I? I don't want
drugs, I don't want to walk or tone down the roaring something

makes in my throat. Between waves I talk to the thrumming
smaller heart trapped between my bones. Nothing to say but come.
What comes is icy water rising from pubis to navel, with needles
crashing and sinking in my lower spine—why don't I just break?

They say natural light is leaking back into the world, they say
thirty-six hours, they say surgery—and we slide down a long tube
to a place with blood on the floor, to a hand slicing a neat slit
along the path they shaved, a thin-lipped mouth in my belly

that smiles in their hands and belches out a loud pinkness,
ancient and tenacious, flapping for all she's worth,
until they plop her on my chest where she closes her beak
on the grub that is my nipple, and I am anything but empty.

Gone Fishin'

Fatigue has turned my blood to honey, sweet dream
of sleep, tiny creatures battening down my eyelids
at strictly the most inopportune times—
a high curb on the right, a darting blue van
on the left, and me as dull as a tarp
or in the middle of *Little Bear's Visit* suddenly
a word dissolving on the page and a child
staring up into my foolish blank face.
People who wear fatigues must get very tired—
Those steep walls they scale, and all the metal they carry!
Here at someone else's desk I tire of my hat,
a metaphor of authority perched on my part.
Ink pools on paper, a deep shrug wanders
my underground at a snail's pace.
Sometimes the rubber wedge holding the door open is
nudged aside, sometimes I stand on the high
balding riverbank and dive in cleanly.
Mostly I step backwards into the current and sleep comes
to meet me from behind, slowly rising water.
When the wet envelope is sealed over the crown
of my head, I am sucked into the half-light,
I snore and drool, I join the rush to the sea. . .

We Live in Bodies

That we do means everything to me now
as I try to sort you out try to imagine
sticking you in the ground veins
drained or bones burned to dust try
to imagine what will be left here
in my lap empty hands mind's eye
my cup of having to go on

We live in bodies clumsy and disobedient
and we love them even as we punish
with too much or too little
we think we're bigger than they are
and then we sit dumbly surprised
how easily that tiny jot of spirit can get lost
so many folds of yellow and pink tissue

There are those who have looked back looked down
from ceilings of hospital rooms and returned to us
we see their lips full and red again but their words
hover fleshless in vowels and consonants
our heads nod yes our bones say no because living
in bodies means blood in all its horror and beauty
means making each other hum and ooze making
baby bodies means we can lay our hands on their
bodies where and when we must not
as we age our bodies pale with the knowing

The fact of sagging flesh and bodily regrets
the fact of slowly applied pain the hand somewhere
applying it while in this latitude her small mouth
tugs and closes over my nipple
the power of a shriek the solace of singing
winding our twisted sinewy streets
bodies are the doomed and wonderful cities where we live

THREE

Now That the Fields

Now that the fields belong to the crows
and the dark rolls in on a cart with supper,
we thicken the skin of the house, tuck a caterpillar
of hay, a reverse moat, around the foundation.

Half the crickets in Conway died last night
under cold rocks—or do they all go at once, once
chainsaws are oiled and this new air reeks of apples?
Now that the last chrysalis has refused to open and our ears

are full of frantic roadwork, emergencies are blooming
like chrysanthemums—four in one weekend: first a heart
forgets the rhythm, then a woman leaps a ditch and hears
a loud crack in one of her body's branches; one man falls off

his roof, another sits up and says: *Breathing is just too hard*,
now that the leaves are blushing to see their true selves
and the flies droning their *I told you so* song.
One blazing maple has taken over the town.

Funny How

Funny how the breeze on my skin does its ruffling thing
with my thoughts. Not quite affectionate. Funny how

staring at the rug I tattoo the floor, thinking if my hair
were thicker maybe I'd like convertibles and other

big wind. Tonight you're away and I'm happy filling the bed
with such teasing itinerant notions, easy to love and let go.

Until the sound: the flat click of the kitchen door
brings metal to my mouth. Something from the driveway

is in the house—looking for what? I have my voice at hand
and the body that wants to use it as a shield, an elephant

behind a sapling. Funny how all that I am is lying here,
a sweating piece of meat. Where is the maxim to unlock

my throat, how can I throw the pillar-of-salt I'm made of
over my left shoulder? I'd like a wrap of music please. This

is the time for a small earthquake, an insomniac neighbor—
any old clatter to put intruder fear to flight. But if he's real,

if tonight is marked for crime, please let me wake tomorrow
simply to find a hole where the TV was, chops thrown

from the freezer. Honey, come home. Don't leave me here
waiting for some gloved hand holding polaroids of my nakedness.

I'm stuck in a child self under stale cloth, an old dream breathing
down my neck: the man without a face, all skin beneath a gray hat.

I need to know what's on the other side of that door,
the baldest reading of terror, the only way home.

A Hotel by Any Other Name

Love—even forbidden love—doesn't deserve linoleum,
doesn't expect to pay cash up front to an experienced
frown behind bullet-proof glass, but this magnetism
is discovered on the fly, in a city neither can claim.
Not sure how to get their hands into the act but knowing

it will happen, they walk, boiling down their lives,
comparing reactions to curbside offerings and molting
neighborhoods, nibbling nuts and the idea of other.
Forty blocks, fifty, and they are as good as undressed.
Laughing, they watch their shoes lead them here, to hotel

resolute, hotel no-nonsense on the square: no luggage, no soap,
no telling. They don't need a lobby with "Moon River."
They pump their bodies like the necks of young swans,
gleeful to sweat on bad beds under worse art, mopping their
sweet new juice with holey towels thin as the walls,

which all night amplify moaning and showers, fisticuffs
and redemption. None of it pedigreed, all of it audible,
Memorex, like their love. A hotel in the middle of otherwise,
which will stand—squat and sure on this rubbled and unsuspecting
street and nowhere else, it will stand, clapping.

May at the Agway

Baby turkeys in their feathers and long legs
and a black flop-eared dog with his nose in the box
tail madly wagging beside the gnarled dirt-creased
hands of the chicken-farmer with blue-gray curls who drives
a black and yellow pickup but does not keep bees
though she gives advice about setting hens in the Agway
on a lark, off to buy white shoes and get a fishing
license and reads Melville and her husband doesn't like
white shoes or turkeys because they don't even know how to
mate by themselves but he reads Michener and dreams of
palm trees and leaving the backhoe behind and says forget
the fishing license, let's apply for passports even if
the world isn't safe for Americans, you got to play the
percentages and it's our turn for palm trees and
meanwhile I know his wife would sell me good pullets
but I want to know why instead of bingo she likes
beautiful stamps and real silk because these people
are beginning to confuse me with their hot tips on local
restaurants and aspirations and my own ten hens and one
cock don't seem so exotic even if I do write poems because
she doesn't knit and he doesn't ignore her in fact
he knows a lot more than turkeys do and if I buy manure
from them at least now I don't think I need to water it like
I used to which I guess says anyone of us can spring loose

How Animals Do It

51

The Egg

Weeding the asparagus, Paul finds a rosy agate egg
six inches down and wonders how it came to cradle there,
bought with colored money bearing many zeroes in a shop
on Rua Maestro Lobo, nestled among clothes bound for home
with framed butterflies and soapstone fish and placed
in a straw-lined box, a lesson to the hens who fussed
and flurried it out and down into the underfoot dung
to lie dormant as only stone knows how, manure rising
to its shoulders by the year, until a shovel pried loose its damp
and pungent dreaming, dumping it a few feet south to feed
the fresh green spears we devour lovingly one month each year
and this immigrant seed that bears no fruit grows now
in my hand, which knows no way to separate smoothness
from pleasure, knows this is no dead thing when I rub
its pink aureole and wake to an inner aching, something
we both can agree upon, this egg in the hand of a woman,
breast in the hand of a man, a lesson not in selflessness
but self, the opposite of hollow.

Yolk

One, two, three—is the ring of chairs around our daily
table the right size? Is it time to stretch open
or do right by? Is the operative term underfoot,
undercapitalized, or under duress?
Every room seems to have a ceiling mirror
and here we are: dressed up, dressed down,
hand to mouth, a spray of lonesome hair, a tuft
of camaraderie, a swag of hope, crown of thorns.
Are we headed for Lake Dry Dock or a wide green
barge on the Nile? If I had to choose,
what would I wish inside me from this month's love?
A stray fragrance, ravaged memory, safe
echo? Or a swoon of repeating cells,
an undertow of more? I'm not sure I can
look up from my plate. This morning's yolk
is glowing around a jot, a tiny knob of the possible
and my lap is yellow with longing.

American Train

Passengers, traveling as light as we can
and alone. No phonecalls, disc jockeys, icebox hum—
that familiar static.
Instead: rows and rows of clumsy black shoes,
random and shruggingly insistent
like backyards in winter—why
don't they cover themselves up?
If only there was snow in the air,
if only we'd brought needle and thread
to reinforce that loose button.
We can't look up: strangers
who might resemble memories
wobble past down the aisle.

The tracks thunder ahead and behind,
a flashy two-way street, willful
and precarious, blasted through rockface
which whispers: *manmade, manmade.*
We're somehow ridiculous
with our waxpaper bags, our knitting
in the face of the imperturbable world.
The clouds just don't care
if they get out of whack, nor the trees,
throwing up their hands in the air,
because we're leaving them a little at a time.

Once

For once we let the world move
through yellow light, watching high arcs
loose in treetops. And the river, it turns out,
always does what it does, and lazily.
Whispers *Don't jump* to dark figures on the bridge.
Reclines, like you, in a bath of moving shadow
(but you'd be thinking *Jump*, eager as I am).
The quality of light, you said. Once.
Small movements on a stationary axis
are permitted: an ear cocked to the peepers
(all around us in the trees),
a peek through opera glasses backwards
(a 19th century landscape painting!),
a safe lean out over the edge
trying to decipher submerged leaves,
suicide notes no one gets to cry over.
When the sky gets done throwing down its orange rays
strands of cloud drift downwind on the water:
the river clears its throat. One whoosh
and the leaves all tear themselves away at once,
swarms of reckless color joining the rush downriver:
peanut shells, runaway laundry, the bottle
bearing our message—*thanks*—all light things
that have been heaved or unhinged at the right moment.
Just a bunch of birds let loose into darkness.

Inevitable Postcards

1

All along I have this feeling: memory
struggling to dash off a postcard—you know,
the clear-skyed, tantalizing kind,
long on vistas, short on information.
Sound: man chopping wood.
Could be just out of sight of a campfire,
kids jumping through brush looking
for marshmallow sticks, he'll help them later.
Now there's just him and the axe.

2

It's disturbing not to know
which sounds are closest: silverware
being rattled, doors opening
and closing, you breathing in your chair.
This ventriloquist trick of other people's lives
setting perspective on its ear.
What are walls for, after all?

3

Postcard: two women in old-fashioned bathing dresses,
lifting and squeezing the hems, self-conscious smiles,
they can almost see their grey-stockinged legs
ankle-deep in the tide.   Yes, their heads are wrapped,
bandaged almost, in dull cloth.   And of course
that's a sailing ship tiny in the background,
clouds cruising the sky.   But what I like is the number—
9653—as if there were many others,
and the inscription: "Wringing wet."

4

Why don't we write each other love poems?
Look at me collapse into babysobs and bare need, me,
sturdy and self-sufficient. We must know more
than we're willing to say, wordlessly
taking our tender spots out for air,
then setting them on fire. It's hard
for our simpleton hearts to understand
a love that's broken in, dependable,
a gift without wheels. And what if I wake
distracted, carting back from sleep some stray,
persistent dream: an arm thrown towards me, electric,

slightly off the beat?   Sometimes my pockets bulge
with little scenarios that leave you out.
What's our love made of then?

5

We're in each other's hands.
A single, irrefutable postcard, the kind
with no picture, saying simply
"I'm staying." Make love larger—
it is large. Find a metaphor—for what?
Maybe it's most of all like painting a scene
you're in the middle of: you'd have to recede
for a view of the whole, and who
would willingly leave the center?

FOUR

Broken Railings

Why do I love broken railings, a couple of steel teeth
knocked out and broken cable like scarecrow hands
pointing to somebody's fall.
I want things whole but I love things broken.
I study the photograph: crumbs of concrete
flaking white, metal rods exposed, all of it
strangely beautiful on a green road in Brazil.
Inside the plywood box the newly laid egg
lies delicately cracked in the straw.
Somebody went over that railing.   He's on a long table.
Then they heft him from a cold metal drawer and lay him
on velvet.   There is no gentleness in the room.
The cows are out again.   The youngest are always first,
spritely or small enough to avoid the crackling wires.
Then the heavy-hooved mothers, who bellow, eat our roses.
One leans into the fence so hard it decides to splinter.
We herd them back.   We have a beer.   We wonder
about the moment of our death.   The membrane protecting us
useless as shards of bottles on high cement walls
against thieves.   The beauty of beach glass, chipped
porcelain, bone fragments when they're dry and clean.
The sun glinting on all our mistakes.
Instead of going back to bed the ex-assistant treasury
secretary stands in his third-floor bedroom and imagines
running full tilt at the back fence, sees himself
hurtling at the air and whacking the top rail so hard
it turns to toothpicks.   He'd be on the other side.
The rooster crows.   Nails a hen.   Ten minutes later
the ex-assistant treasury secretary is standing on the lawn
in the wet early light and the hen is grunting an egg
down a tight pink chute.   The cows are still in the pasture
sitting in their pools of nose vapor.
The picture is too beautiful.
There are ripples distorting the lake.

In Brazil the red clay tumbles down a hillside
and someone on the early morning milk run sees the crack
in the road that will open large enough by ten
to accommodate a whole bus.
People will be broken and their people broken
for a long time after. Most of them
will never lie on velvet, even when they're cold
cows under the field. It makes no sense
in this world to love things broken.
The ex-assistant treasury secretary hugs this thought
as if it were his own. He puts the gun in his mouth,
cold metal, perfect as an egg. I look up thinking
"Three's way too many. One of these roosters has to go."
When a man handed me a jewelry box he'd made of a violin case
carefully lined with soft velvet compartments
I set the thing on the floor.
I saw a baby coffin. It lives under the spare bed.
It's scary to think of dying in your sleep.
I want to know when I go. When the pager asleep
in the grass comes to life and the crackly voice says
"gunshot" I drop the trowel and pull rubber gloves
over caked dirt. Do I love things broken?
Can these hands make anything whole?
I pull the elastic on the back of the oxygen mask gently
over a patch of wet hair: bone with dry tines
like a wooden fork long buried in the backyard,
half unearthed now in my lap. The lake goes calm.
Every fence in town holds its breath.
Across my sweatshirt big blue letters spell "Heaven" and
I'm hoping the ex-assistant treasury secretary didn't see
or that he possessed a wonderful dark humor.
I'm hoping we'll all get home tonight. I'm hoping
he's somewhere, whole.

Mama What's a Gulf?

Before my daughter's third birthday I'd never heard of a Scud
I hadn't thought about the little leaves of January
brown claws on their knuckles skittering across the road

I'd never had to explain *friendly fire* to a child
or a president smiling as he declared war
I didn't know that certain nerve cells have megaphones

didn't know that the stones and wisps of ribbon
the sunglasses fallen from grace in the top drawer
all those bunged-up unstrung things have words for us

or that one moment one persimmon two teacups
could make a certain difference
if only we spoke the language and had the right change

This business of chance has me balled up in knots
warm sleep-tossed children in a cold sleepless world
I didn't know bad people could mean well

I knew my way around but the room was small and had no door
the desert so vast and nowhere to hang my hat
Tracer rounds pearls of the night

light up the four a.m. couch littered with chips
light up the abyss between afghans and gas masks
At the first daylight bombings the doves are flying wildly confused

The Edge of the Wild

Wilderness has no roads, ergo you and I have never
seen it, though we have faith it's shrinking, know
we'd like it, write checks to protect it, this idea
thought up indoors. Big-hearted, we live on the fringes,
trap groundhogs, poison moles, applaud volunteer
vegetables in our happy garden. We sigh and point
to the small bodies on the road's shoulders, I feel lucky
when the chipmunk makes it through the spokes
of my bike. Behind our backyard is field, then forest
and forest, too familiar to be wilderness. Like a
campground, we have stopped the true wild
from happening here, though it creeps close as we sleep.
Eats our cats, snip snap, in the form of a fisher.
We still like the coyotes' racket on the far hill, but now
we hear teeth in their song. A bear at the beehive,
a cub in the cornflakes—these stories paint our way out
of hours and closed doors. We feel helpful, bringing
a flattened possum to preschool; the children circle
with paintbrushes, touching without touching, hands
and faces clean. We're not sure about the ethics
of zoos. Meanwhile, the neighbors are up in arms—
Doc's guinea hens shriek and crap and wander; grown
too wild to herd, they must be shot out of the trees.
A little boy emerges from the safety of the house:
Daddy, where is its head, did it turn to air? His daddy
is eager to talk about war, where the boy thinks
only the stupid die. I have a scar where someone's dog
tore back my lip; I stood, disbelieving, bleeding
into the tablescraps. They offered aloe, drove me
to Emergency, but they did not *put him down*
or any other euphemism. Did he forget who he was?
Too much ease can do that. But then it is the rich
and lucky who get to walk away from all they have made
to the edge of the wild sometimes, sit on a rock

no one owns. As if it's there for us to see.
And after watching all the busyness in nature's big
bowl, the way we stutter guilty through our lives
armed with lists and beepers looks plain silly.
Other creatures have mantras—MAKE BABIES or
WINTER'S COMING—and they *do* the thing
without a fuss, unless distracted by the perfect flat
rock in the sun, unless someone eats them first.

Volunteer

My pager tells me a disagreeable man
is having trouble breathing but I don't turn back.
This day has a destination.
The house I'm heading for is like an iceberg,
more underground than above.
There is a man pulling at his cartoon
shirt, his face is an oil painting.
The mouth is a smudge.
I'm sorry, but I'm more sorry
because I like him.
In the picture on the table a tall-masted ship
—who in his right mind would have named her HOPE?—
is going down in polar ice. I'm pretty sure
this is not my responsibility. Last week, it took me
eight minutes to get to the ambulance, I'm not ready
to tell why. Behind the dark ruin, insistent
dailiness. A weasel is sucking blood, one chicken
per night, but I sleep undisturbed.
It's the underlayer sneaking up.
It's the smudge factor.
It's the shards of solid cold I can do nothing about.
The stubble on the hillside is okay with me,
it's the way the front step is gone.
It's the great chunks of flooring in frigid water
that say: you're seizing up, you're going down.
The teeth say, the hands say.
The house does not say come, it says
stand and stare if you must but please cover my legs.
Eight minutes
deciding if someone's emergency
was enough.

Beauty, Aching

I'm driving back roads the day the sap buckets
come down in Massachusetts, a sweet sloshing
and clanking that marks the way we inch forward,

or do we walk backwards as we cast lingering glance
after glance, hoping not to stumble into the idea
of our deaths? WATERWAYS GIVE UP GRIM TELLTALE

SIGNS OF SPRING says the headline on the seat—
half the bloated bodies of the year dragging
their cinderblocks to the surface this month

of first greening, some with time still clicking
on their wrists. So why is the muddy world so
full of beauty, aching? Even awful knowledge

blooms with things that snag us—we dangle
above the river, gawking. And if my sweet calico
made a meal for coyotes? And if women shiver

to see antennas and men shy from shears and we all
make words dangerous? Still a fox can hear a worm
across a field, still the wind makes its dust

from stone, and I can't not laugh at that house
sitting on a hill like a fat queen on a throne,
and I'm so lucky I can go home to the sprawled

girl of seven rearranging magnetic words to say to no
one in particular: "A thousand poles above the diamond
fall, our meanest mist turns in the living sky."

The Feather

for A.W.

You stand alone like the cheese in the song,
encircled, adrift, a bird in your throat
and your palms a flapping shield before your face.
For three years you have worked toward naming the why.
Under your tight cap of hair sits your story, hunched over
and lonely as you are.   Self-preservation forbids you
to befriend it, you meet only in dreams.
The toddler in your lap is a din, a face crying *Now!*
You imagine her silenced many different ways.
One day when you wake, the red imprint of a man's hand:
memory tattooed on your thigh. On your blood you swear
this girl child will know love in her bones
and own the key to her body.
You are a woman, not a squaw but a brave.
You wear your feather with a vengeance.
The quill of it drilled into the soft cup of flesh
at the root of speech, at the crux of breath.
At the precise fork of who you are.
Something you own is hurtling its way
to where you can see it.
You twist the feather in place, your fingers find
the exit wound at the back of your neck, stroke the tip
proud in its red crown of flesh.
The ink begins to flow.

Common Crows

Better to be common crows with diplomas they said
than to bicker among the more colorful relations
purposeless on their dark branch

No railroad tracks in our family but the aunts
and uncles still lived on the wrong side
the ones with fewer male offspring than cars
on blocks the ones we saw a few rare Sundays
in their tattoos on their turf only because one uncle
drove nowhere his day off from driving bus because
the other went nowhere there was no beer
because they'd just as soon tuck dry bills
into birthday cards and leave it at that but we preacher's kids
we needed a cautionary tale twice yearly and dark
as the road to Damascus was blinding

We sat with our hands in our laps shy before women
with painted eyebrows bruised arms
we jiggled our plastic tumblers of stale ice cubes
eyeing mysterious holes punched in the walls
cousins born smoking and swaggering Bill and Kay's
little Billy and little Kay and Linda the good one
who married badly cousins who squinted and crouched
shooting plates off the wainscotting who
got knocked up or knocked off bowling alleys
dyed their roots or did time

Years later like in a bad novel the move
to the trailer the sunken cheekbones the mouth
sewn shut into a long thin scar
like in a novel the fire Aunt Kay burnt
black as her hair uncles like boats
with no moorings and Nana convinced TV's
should have window shades they look
straight at me when I take off my slip

We see them now only at funerals these
nieces with whom we share jaw lines cousins
with rare conditions putty-colored aunts
who knew the preacher when
he was a machinist and liked him more

Blood kin without bootstraps or travel trailers
who sweep up or hose down whose cheesy socks
some long ago holiday we inhaled
sleeping head to toe on the sofa bundled two
to a bathtub of blankets all the relatives I let slide
down the chute to the cellar of my homemade
house of self

Brought up on mashed potatoes wild to be anything
but bland jealous of four-syllable names
from foreign tongues anyone with a past compressed
like coal to what could be carried on their backs
I look for my ethnicity and find it
in the ones we were better than

Glen Cove, 1957

A strawberry shortcake sits breathing sweetness on a cloud
      above the curvy cartoon fridge and I am seven climbing
phone books piled on a wobbly chair until the dull silver
      radiator looms, then a trickle and someone saying
cracked open. Am I dead? Am I an egg? I hatch out,
      bandaged under grapevines near a gullyful of trash.
The wooden lawn chair knits splinters into the backs of my
      knees and I will get no shortcake. Am I downcast or
defiant? This and so much else I reach for is gone—
      the color of the bulkhead being painted,
the kind of sandwiches my mother hands the splattered
      churchmen, and does she know she's pretty?
Rotten apples on spring ground are smeary bittersweet
      and I am the age of my daughter who still loves fog.
I hate it. The way last month's huge sadnesses and tiny
      triumphs are leaking onto her pillow as she sleeps,
and who knows which moments will get snagged and remain
      to point to who she's become once she's forgotten
the rest, her right foot asleep and her daughter
      gap-mouthed below her wide with the world.

Innocence and Air

Snow drifting the mud, the first day we can drive
with the car windows open, and from the back seat:
"It's slashing me, Mama!"
"Splashing you?"
"No, slashing."
"That sounds violent" (my knitted brow).
"It is violet, sort of."
The preferred color of her fifth year.
"This is great—" she says,
"—the wind just swallowed my ear."

Where the Dead Live

The dead live in all the spaces
we live-wires don't think big enough
for the size of our loss.
Here. A crescent eyelash on my fingertip,
shockingly black—that's my aunt, always dramatic.
There's a grandmother in the moment
between rocking chair still and rocking chair
rocking. Here, in my arms, a baby
dead with a hole in her heart each time
I let Della out of my sight.
A thin old man with a sharp tongue
sits with his legs crossed like a woman
in every tool I ever hold in my hand or even see in another's.

Our dead may not have planned it this way but they've left
stains on recipes: lemons squeezed in 1965 in a kitchen
unrecognizable now but for the black cat clock,
its tail still twitching time. What about the uncle
in a shiny salesman's suit who could build you a house
with his bare hands: he lives in the split second
before laughter, buying rounds for strangers in the HuKeLau.

Whether I like it or not, there's a moon-faced
Humpty Dumpty of a grampa, a bad father and a bad drunk,
who lives in all white food, finally puréed and forgiven,
if not understood. And the long, twisted face,
the one-breasted wife who outlived him,
who gave up her chair to whoever walked in the room—
she's in a sharp smell I never remember until it's there
and I catch myself wondering who she might have become if.

Then there's the tiny beat of a drum when you and I
discover we're headed for love, a soft sound
walled off as in a frame, and suddenly between us

a square little head, a pair of hands clamped
around a wooden car, thumbtacks for hubcaps,
and just as our grown-up hands find all the right places
we know it's the little boy we made but never met.
The dead don't flake off like so much shed skin.

The dead live in our mouths.   Don't we sometimes open them
without knowing why?   It's because they're there
in the wood grain of every bone-tired threshold we cross,
every shop window we pass, catching their reflection in ours,
in the taxi that pulls to the curb and flings its doors at us
and without knowing what we'll find left on the back seat
we know it's ours and it's time to step inside.

Tenderness

writes *You* bigger than *I* it's the kiss that doesn't wake
    the sleeper the pink knot in a chest filled to bursting
        refusing intrusive surgery learning
            simply to glow—tenderness

is the placing of much more inside very much but gently
    so as not to capsize the boat it's closer to contentment
        than ecstasy low-priced enough to be easily lost
            remember from the train at dusk the last things

with color are the strangler vines well the beauty of tenderness
    is you can close your eyes to see it passion needs a mirror
        has been known to buy a one-way ticket
            in our happiest moments we vanish from our sight

World Greater Than We Make

ruin: total destruction or disintegration
rendering something formless, useless, or
valueless
            —*American Heritage Dictionary*

1

The ruin I'm thinking of spilled down the entire hillside,
blocks of stone like dice shaken in the cup of the sky.
A place that invites whispering or song. Darkly inviting
as the slaughterhouse collapsed beside a lonely road.
Crazed china, the lightning-bolt symmetry of cracks.
A ruin is the bones of a thing slowly exposed by time,
wind, water. The fin of an old Caddy rusting in a circle
of trees on a high ridge. The ribs of a boat
rocking on sand. Colors only waiting can paint.
All gashes are old gashes. No blood.

2

I wander Manaus, city of perpetual ruin,
where the walls grow new layers all by themselves,
where a man sits writing a novel neither of us knows
I will translate eight years later. I am alone
and inexplicably happy. I lean back off the curb
into traffic to fill my eyes with the grand,
decayed façade, spindly papaya trees
at attention in second-story windows.
I bend to the gutter for a chip of tile, twirl it
under my chin like a buttercup: it says
I love this accident.

3

The dictionary is dead (and it was a good one): the ruin
is spilling still. The farthest thing from worthless,
it is a sadness made beautiful over time—or is it beauty
made sad? A silent clash of meanings we can

picnic in. We say a lot about ourselves
with the buildings we build, but their ruins speak
with other than human voices. See how ruins gladly
join earth and sky, how the natural world bends down, creeps in,
to meet them. More fools we, to preserve or reconstruct
the stone and wood we borrow, instead of simply watching
as gorgeous chaos slowly gathers back its own.

Notes

Circa 1970, page 24:

The first (and repeating) line echoes Carol Potter's poem "Herding the Chickens" (*Before We Were Born*,
Alice James Books, 1990).

Liza, page 31:

In memory of Liza Kornstadt Ouimette (1990-1991).

Hungry for Them, page 34:

In Portuguese, a child's mother and godmother refer to each other as *Comadre* (co-mother).

Tenderness, page 75:

I am indebted to Andrei Sinyavsky for the last line.

Recent Titles by Alice James Books

ALICE JAMES BOOKS has been publishing poetry since 1973. One of the few presses in the country that is run collectively, the cooperative selects manuscripts for publication through competitions. New authors become active members of the press, participating in editorial and production activities. The press, which places an emphasis on publishing women poets, was named for Alice James, sister of William and Henry, whose gift for writing was ignored and whose fine journal did not appear until after her death.